habitat explorer

Ocean Explorer

Greg Pyers

www.raintreepublishers.co.uk
Visit our website to find out more information about **Raintree** books.

To order:
☎ Phone 44 (0) 1865 888112
📄 Send a fax to 44 (0) 1865 314091
💻 Visit the Raintree Bookshop at **www.raintreepublishers.co.uk** to browse our catalogue and order online.

Published in 2004 by Heinemann Library
a division of Harcourt Education Australia,
18–22 Salmon Street, Port Melbourne Victoria 3207 Australia
(a division of Reed International Books Australia Pty Ltd,
ABN 70 001 002 357).
Visit the Heinemann Library website @
www.heinemannlibrary.com.au

First published in Great Britain by Raintree,
Halley Court, Jordan Hill, Oxford OX2 8EJ,
part of Harcourt Education.
Raintree is a registered trademark of Harcourt Education Ltd.

ℛ A Reed Elsevier company

© Reed International Books Australia Pty Ltd 2004
First published in paperback in 2005

ISBN 1 74070 143 7 (hardback)
08 07 06 05 04
10 9 8 7 6 5 4 3 2 1

ISBN 1 84443 467 2 (paperback)
09 08 07 06 05
10 9 8 7 6 5 4 3 2 1

Editorial: Carmel Heron, Sandra Balonyi
Design: Stella Vassiliou, Marta White
Photo research: Legend Images, Wendy Duncan
Production: Tracey Jarrett
Map: Guy Holt
Diagram: Andy Craig & Nives Porcellato

Typeset in Officina Sans 19/23 pt
Pre-press by Digital Imaging Group (DIG)
Printed in China by WKT Company Limited

National Library of Australia Cataloguing-in-Publication data:
Pyers, Greg.
    Ocean explorer.

    Bibliography.
    Includes index.
    For primary school students.
    ISBN 1 74070 143 7 (hardback)
    ISBN 1 84443 467 2 (paperback)

    1. Marine ecology – Juvenile literature. I. Title.
    (Series: Pyers, Greg. Habitat explorer).

Acknowledgements
The publisher would like to thank the following for permission to reproduce photographs:

APL/Corbis: p. 12; APL/Minden: pp. 8, 11, 28; Auscape/OSF: pp. 4, 27, /Francois Gohier: pp. 6, 24, 25, /Mark Spencer: p. 9, Jean-Paul Ferrero: pp. 15, 23, /D. Parer & E. Parer-Cook: p. 18, /Kevin Deacon: p. 19, /Ian Gordon: p. 20; CSIRO: p. 29; Getty Images: p. 22; © IN2P3/CNRS, Antares: p. 16; photolibrary.com: pp. 7, 10, 13, 17, 26; photolibrary.com/OSF: p. 14.

Cover photograph of a Pacific Spotted Dolphin reproduced with permission of APL/CJ Watt.

Every attempt has been made to trace and acknowledge copyright. Where an attempt has been unsuccessful, the publisher would be pleased to hear from the copyright owner so any omission or error can be rectified.

Contents

Any words appearing in the main text in bold, **like this**, are explained in the Glossary.

The Pacific Ocean

Imagine you are on a beach of a tiny island, looking out to sea. From this viewpoint, the ocean seems to be an empty place. There are no plants to be seen and the only animals you can see are a pair of gulls flying in to land. But the ocean teems with life. To explore the ocean fully, you will need to go beneath the surface.

Explorer's notes

Ocean description:
- salty air
- gulls calling
- waves swelling
- foam crashing.

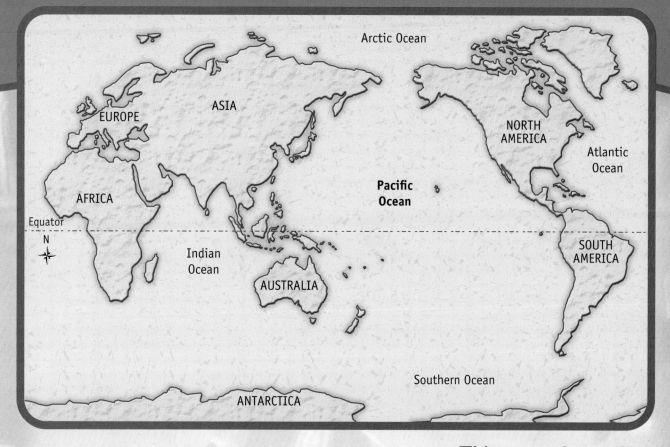

The map labels:

Arctic Ocean

EUROPE

ASIA

NORTH AMERICA

Atlantic Ocean

AFRICA

Pacific Ocean

Equator

N

Indian Ocean

AUSTRALIA

SOUTH AMERICA

Southern Ocean

ANTARCTICA

Pacific habitats

The Pacific Ocean covers 155 million square kilometres. There are deep seas and shallow seas. Within this vast expanse, there are many **habitats** – places where animals and plants live. Habitats of the sea are called **marine** habitats. One kind of marine habitat is the ocean surface, but hidden beneath it are many more.

This maps shows the locations of the world's oceans. The Pacific Ocean includes the cold seas of the far north and far south, and the warm tropical seas along the equator.

An alien world

Humans are not suited to living in the ocean. Unlike **marine** animals, we do not have the features that would help us survive there. These features are called **adaptations**. But, with the right equipment, you can overcome this problem – at least partly. You put on your **scuba** swimming gear and enter the water ...

Seeing underwater

Marine animals, such as seals, have eyes with special lenses that make everything clear underwater. With your goggles on, your underwater view is also made clear.

Adaptations

Water is difficult to move through. It is 800 times denser than air. Many marine animals, such as fish, have a streamlined shape. This helps them to slip through the water. Many also have fins or flippers which push the water aside and propel them along. The flippers you wear on your feet will help you swim.

To breathe, you have to carry a tank of oxygen on your back with a hose connecting it to your mouth. Fish can absorb oxygen straight from the water, through their **gills**.

While fish are at home underwater, a human needs special equipment even for a short visit.

Explorer's notes

SCUBA stands for:
self-
contained
underwater
breathing
apparatus.

Shallow seas

You are at the very edge of the ocean, where land meets sea. The water is shallow here – no more than 20 metres deep. Sunlight reaches all the way to the sea floor. All plants need light to grow and with so much light, there are many plants here. Just ahead of you is a forest of the largest **marine** plants of all: giant kelp.

A kelp forest provides food and shelter for many animals.

Kelp forest

Hundreds of kelp plants, most more than 15 metres tall, are growing side by side. Each consists of straps and ribbons attached to a flexible stem. The stem is anchored to a rocky reef below by a part called a **holdfast**. The straps and ribbons are like the leaves of a land plant catching sunlight to make sugars. Gas-filled bladders along the kelp's stem act like tiny floats to keep the plant upright and close to the sunlight.

Gas-filled bladders can be seen on these kelp stems.

Explorer's notes

Kelp **adaptations**:
- gas bladders
- holdfast
- flexible stem
- straps and ribbons.

Ocean skies

Shallow coastal waters are only a tiny part of the **marine** environment. Most of the ocean is too deep for **scuba** diving. So, now you board a boat and head far from land, out to the open ocean.

It is quiet out here. It seems a very lonely place. But then you see that you have company.

Gannets

Gannets are large sea birds that catch fish by diving head-first into the sea from 30 metres up. Gannets return to land to roost after each day's fishing.

This young wandering albatross will travel several hundred thousand kilometres in its lifetime of 40 years or more.

Albatross

A huge bird is gliding around and over the boat. It is a wandering albatross, among the largest of all flying birds. Its wings stretch 3 metres from tip to tip. These carry the bird for weeks on end over the open ocean, hardly flapping the whole time. When the bird has filled its **crop** with fish, it will return to its mate waiting far away on an island in the Southern Ocean.

Explorer's notes

Albatross features:
- long, narrow wings
- large, powerful beak
- large, webbed feet.

11

Ocean surface

The boat bobs like a cork on the ocean surface. You're not used to this constant movement and it makes you feel a little ill. Suddenly, a large, dark shape appears just below the surface. It is a basking shark, the world's second-largest fish, and it is feeding on **plankton**.

In one hour, enough water passes through the basking shark's gills to fill a large swimming pool.

Plankton

Plankton are microscopic plants and animals that drift on the ocean currents. The plant plankton (**phytoplankton**) uses sunlight to grow, so it floats near the ocean surface. The animal plankton (**zooplankton**) is found there too, because it eats phytoplankton.

These zooplankton, called amphipods, can be viewed under a microscope.

Basking sharks feed by opening their huge mouths and swimming slowly. Seawater flows in and passes out through the shark's **gills**. Special body parts called gill rakers filter the plankton from the water.

Oxygen producers

Most of the world's oxygen is produced by phytoplankton. Like all plants, phytoplankton use sunlight to produce sugars from water and carbon dioxide. Oxygen is produced during this process.

Krill and krill-eaters

The water has turned a pink colour. Small birds called prions are fluttering over the water and snatching at it with their beaks. Suddenly, the birds scatter. The water begins to swirl. Bubbles break the surface. Something is about to happen...

The giant gaping mouth of a blue whale erupts from the sea. Seconds later, it disappears beneath the waves. The sea falls quiet and the pinky stain has gone.

Blue whales

An adult blue whale may weigh up to 130 tonnes and measure 30 metres in length. It is the largest animal ever to have lived. Whales are **mammals** and feed their young milk. A blue whale calf drinks 500 litres of milk a day.

Whale food

The pinky stain was formed by a type of **zooplankton** called krill. Krill resemble tiny prawns. They are the main food of **baleen** whales, such as the blue whale. These whales use their tongues to force seawater through the baleen that hangs from their jaws. The krill are trapped and swallowed. A single blue whale may eat 3.5 tonnes of krill a day.

A swarm of krill consists of millions of individuals like this one, viewed under a microscope.

Explorer's notes

Baleen whales:
- right whales
- humpback whales
- fin whales
- blue whales
- bowhead whales
- sei whales
- minke whales
- Bryde's whales.

In the bathyscaphe

A craft called a **bathyscaphe** (pronounced 'bath-i-scaf') will take you on a journey to the ocean floor, more than six kilometres (four miles) below. You climb aboard through a hatch in the top. When the hatch is sealed tightly, a crane lowers the bathyscaphe over the side and into the sea. The descent is about to begin.

Bathyscaphes

A bathyscaphe is heavily built so that it can withstand the enormous water **pressure** of the ocean depths. It also carries an oxygen supply, and a two-way radio to communicate with the boat above.

This bathyscaphe is being lowered into the sea.

The endless blue

Through a porthole, you have your first underwater view of the open ocean. There is nothing but water in front of you. Out here, there seems to be very little life at all. This is simply because the ocean is so large. It is also because ocean animals do not spread themselves evenly through the ocean.

Fish swim together to find food and to stay safe.

Safety in numbers

A sudden flash of silver is followed by more flashes. And then, as if from nowhere, an enormous **shoal** of herrings emerges from the blue. The fish swirl around each other and then change direction. They move as one, like a huge, shimmering ball. It is impossible to keep your eye on an individual fish.

Anchovy shoals can be so dense that they block out sunlight.

Plankton feeders

Anchovies, sardines and herrings all form enormous shoals. These huge herds of fish roam the ocean surface, feeding on **plankton**. As they go, they attract the attention of **predators**.

Barracudas prey on shoals of plankton feeders.

Predators

Suddenly, the fish crowd even closer together.
A long silver fish darts past, and then another,
and another. A pack of barracudas has arrived.
They circle the shoal. One plunges
into the shoal, with its mouth open
and its teeth bared, but it emerges
without a fish. It will try again,
and again, and soon it will succeed.

Explorer's notes

Food chain:
barracuda
↑
herring
↑
plankton.

Ocean hunters

A lone blue shark has appeared among the barracudas. It begins to feed on the darting herrings. The shark's streamlined shape, powered by a flexible, muscular body and a thrashing tail, enables it to speed up quickly. Its pointed teeth catch the slippery **prey**. But how did it find the shoal in the first place?

A blue shark usually hunts alone.

Echolocation

A dolphin finds prey using **echolocation**. It makes high-pitched clicks that bounce off prey. The dolphin hears the echo and closes in. Dolphins often blow bubbles to surround a shoal like a net, then stun the fish with slaps of their tails.

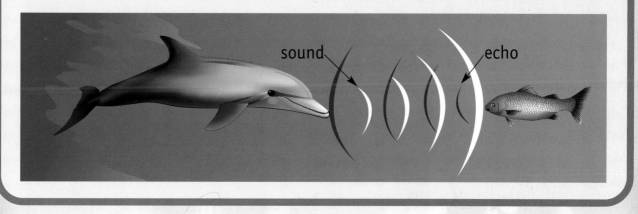

sound

echo

Senses

Sharks can hear the low-pitched sounds of a **shoal** on the move from kilometres away. They can also smell blood in the water from a similar distance. **Predatory** sharks have excellent vision. Their large eyes have pupils that widen in poor light. In total darkness, a shark uses its **electrosense** to find prey. Small **receptors** in the shark's head detect the tiny electrical **impulses** given off by the muscles of prey.

Explorer's notes

Senses used by ocean predators:
- echolocation
- vision
- smell
- hearing
- electrosense.

Colder and darker

The **bathyscaphe** descends. It is **insulated** inside but the thermometer shows that the outside water temperature is falling. The light is beginning to dim as well. At a depth of 100 metres, the sea outside is a twilight world. It is too dark for **phytoplankton** to grow. Dark shapes streak past the porthole. A pod of fur seals is hunting fish.

Steller sea lions can hunt in dim light.

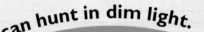

Explorer's notes

Adaptations for hunting in the dark:
- seals – whiskers
- dolphins – **echolocation**
- sharks – **electrosense.**

Staying warm

Mammals, such as seals, have to maintain their warm body temperatures. On land, the thick fur of a seal traps a layer of air close to the animal's skin. Air is an excellent insulator, so the seal loses little heat. But in the cold sea, there is no air, so hair will not keep a seal warm. Instead, a layer of fat, called **blubber**, provides the insulation. Whales and dolphins also have thick layers of blubber.

Seals

Seals use their long whiskers to feel for fish slipping by in the dim light. Seal, dolphin and whale mothers feed their young milk that is ten times fattier than cow's milk. This helps the babies grow their layer of blubber.

Deep divers

By the time the **bathyscaphe** has reached 500 metres, the water outside is near freezing. It is also completely dark. A gauge shows that the ocean is exerting enormous **pressure** on the craft. At this depth, the water pressure is 50 times the air pressure at the surface. At 1500 metres, the water pressure is 150 times the air pressure at the surface. At that depth, a human body would be squashed. But many animals can survive down there.

Explorer's notes

The ocean at 1500 metres depth:
- freezing cold
- completely dark
- enormous pressure
- no plant life.

The bathyscaphe pauses. Its **sonar** has detected something large approaching from above. The outside floodlights are turned on. The craft wobbles. You look through the porthole, straight into the eye of a sperm whale. It is diving. The last you see of the whale is its beating tail, driving it deeper and deeper. The whale is hunting for giant squid, which live only at great depths. The whale may have to dive to 3000 metres in search of its **prey**.

Sperm whales can stay underwater for over an hour.

Ocean floor

The **bathyscaphe** reaches the ocean floor, 4500 metres below the surface. The floodlights are turned off and for a few moments the water looks as black as tar. Then, you notice other lights. Some are blinking on and off, some stay on for a few moments and others flash in sequence from side to side.

Explorer's notes

Species at different depths:
- giant squid – 3000 m
- gulper eel – 4000 m
- hatchet fish – 5000 m
- brotulid (a fish) – 8300 m
- amphipod (a shrimp) – 10 000 m.

The giant squid is the world's largest invertebrate (an animal without a backbone).

Making light

Most of the fish of the deep ocean make their own light to lure **prey**, to startle **predators**, attract mates or to keep together in **shoals**. In most deep ocean fish, it is **bacteria** living in the animal's body that produce the light. The fish turn their lights on and off by opening and closing flaps of skin over the bacteria, or by controlling the blood supply to the bacteria.

Bacteria in the skin of the hatchet fish make this animal glow.

Life at the very bottom

On the floor of the very deepest ocean depths, very few animals can survive. Simple worms and strange shrimps have been found there, sifting through the mud for the tiniest pieces of food that have drifted down from above.

Ocean future

Every year, huge volumes of oil, chemical waste and sewage, and about 100 million tonnes of plastic rubbish, find their way into the world's oceans. This pollution may be washed into the sea from the land, deliberately dumped or washed off ships. It damages **marine habitats** and wildlife.

Marine animals can easily become entangled in plastic rubbish.

Ocean conservation

Protecting the ocean begins on land. That is where much of the pollution comes from. It is also where governments make laws that affect the sea. In many parts of the world, people get together to clean up beaches and to ask governments to protect the sea.

Overfishing

Too much fishing may reduce the numbers of certain fish **species** so much that they may become **extinct**.
For this reason, laws have been made to restrict how much fish can be taken. However, illegal fishing remains a threat to many species.

Orange roughies take many years to mature. If they are overfished they may not breed fast enough to recover.

Explorer's notes

Major threats to the ocean:
- overfishing
- plastics
- pollution.

Find out for yourself

Not many people have the opportunity to explore under the ocean. But there are many places where you can travel by boat to observe whales and other **marine** life such as sea birds. You can also observe the sea from the land. You could keep a diary of which animals you see at different times of the year in the sea.

Using the Internet

Explore the Internet to find out more about ocean **habitats**. Websites can change, so if the link below no longer works, don't worry. Use a kid-friendly search engine, such as www.yahooligans.com or www.internet4kids.com, and type in keywords such as 'marine animals', or even the name of a particular marine animal or plant.

Website

http://www.yoto98noaa.gov/kids.htm
The International Year of Oceans website has links to sites about the world's oceans, including sites with fact sheets, games and videos.

Glossary

adaptation feature of an animal or plant that helps it to survive

bacteria living things consisting of a single cell

baleen hair-like body parts that hang from the upper jaws of baleen whales

bathyscaphe a craft used for exploring the ocean depths

blubber fat

crop food storage pouch in a bird's throat

echolocation finding things by making sounds and listening for the echo

electrosense detection of electricity

extinct when a type of living thing is no longer living

gill body part of a fish that absorbs oxygen from water

habitat place where an animal or a plant lives

holdfast the part of a kelp plant that holds it to a rock

impulse stimulating force

insulate prevent or reduce the loss of body heat

mammal animal that drinks its mother's milk when it is young

marine of the sea

phytoplankton microscopic plants that drift in the sea

plankton tiny animals and plants that drift in the sea

predator animal that kills and eats other animals

pressure force

prey animal that is killed and eaten by other animals

receptors body parts that detect light, heat, electricity and pressure

scuba underwater breathing equipment used by divers

shoal large number or group of fish

sonar system that detects objects underwater using sound

species group of living things that reproduce with each other

tropical of the tropics, the warm regions around the equator

zooplankton microscopic animals that drift in the sea

Index